United States Presidents

George Washington

Anne Welsbacher
ABDO Publishing Company

visit us at
www.abdopub.com

Published by Abdo Publishing Company 4940 Viking Drive, Edina, Minnesota 55435.
Copyright © 1998 by Abdo Consulting Group, Inc. International copyrights reserved in
all countries. No part of this book may be reproduced in any form without written
permission from the publisher.

Printed in the United States.

Cover and Interior Photo credits: Peter Arnold, Inc., SuperStock, Archive, Corbis-
Bettmann

Edited by Lori Kinstad Pupeza
Contributing editors Alan and Elizabeth Gergen

Library of Congress Cataloging-in-Publication Data

Welsbacher, Anne, 1955-
    George Washington / Anne Welsbacher.
    p. cm. -- (United States presidents)
    Summary: A simple biography of the nation's first president, who came to be
known as the "Father of Our Country."
    Includes index.
    ISBN 1-56239-737-0
    1. Washington, George, 1732-1799--Juvenile literature. 2. Presidents--United
States--Biography--Juvenile literature. [1. Washington, George,--1732-1799. 2.
Presidents.] I. Title. II. Series: United States presidents (Edina, Minn.)
    E312.66.W45   1998
    973.4'1'092--dc21
    [B]
                                 97-32923
                                 CIP
                                 AC

Contents

The Father of Our Country

*G*eorge Washington was a leader in the American **Revolution**. The United States fought this war for freedom from England. Because George Washington was such a strong leader, the U.S. won the Revolution and became a free country.

George Washington was a wise leader in battle. He knew when to do bold things and when to hold back. Because he was both brave and careful, his small army trusted him, grew stronger, and won the revolution.

The soldiers who fought with George Washington liked him because he was a strong leader. By the time the war was over, they wanted to make him king of the United States!

After the war, George Washington led a group of men who signed an important paper called the **Constitution**. The Constitution described freedom and rights for Americans.

George Washington portrait.

Later, when the United States needed its first president, everyone chose George Washington!

As a boy, George Washington loved to camp and play in the woods. In school he liked math best. He was best friends with his older half-brother, who taught him many things that helped him as a grown-up.

George Washington married Martha Dandridge Custis. Martha was cheerful and she loved to eat sweets! She went to battlefields with George. She mended soldiers' clothes during the war.

George and Martha did not have children together. But they raised Martha's children from her first marriage. Later, they raised her grandchildren.

George Washington did not even want to be president! He did not think he was smart enough. But everybody else wanted him, so he agreed to the job.

George Washington was careful as a soldier—and as a president. As president, he led the United States through hard times. With his help, Americans learned how to run their new country.

When George Washington retired from being president, he went home to his big farm house, which was called Mt. Vernon. People still loved him and came to visit. Even though George Washington never had children, he is called the father of our country.

George Washington fighting in the American Revolution.

George Washington (1732-1799)
First President

BORN:	February 22, 1732
PLACE OF BIRTH:	Pope's Creek, Westmoreland County, Virginia
ANCESTRY:	English
FATHER:	Augustine Washington (1694-1743)
MOTHER:	Mary Ball Washington (1708-1789)
WIFE:	Martha Dandridge Custis (1731-1802)
CHILDREN:	Adopted two children from his wife's first marriage
EDUCATION:	Private tutors
RELIGION:	Episcopalian
JOBS:	Surveyor, soldier, planter, businessman
MILITARY SERVICE:	Virginia Militia (1753-1758); Commander in Chief of 1st Continental Army (1775-1783)
POLITICAL PARTY:	Federalist

OFFICES HELD:	Member, Virginia House of Burgesses; Delegate to First and Second Continental Congresses; Justice of the Peace for Fairfax County; President of Constitutional Convention
AGE AT INAUGURATION:	57
TERMS SERVED:	Two (1789-1793) (1793-1797)
VICE PRESIDENT:	John Adams (both terms)
DIED:	December 14, 1799, Mount Vernon, Virginia, age 67
CAUSE OF DEATH:	Pneumonia

Detail Area

 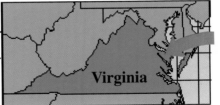

Pope's Creek, Westmoreland County, Virginia

Virginia

Birthplace of George Washington

Early Years

*G*eorge Washington was born at Pope's Creek, Virginia, on February 22, 1732. Virginia was not a state. It was a colony owned by England.

George had five brothers and sisters and two half-brothers from his father's first marriage. When he was three, the family moved to Little Hunting Creek Farm, near the Potomac River in Virginia. George loved exploring the woods and working on the family farm.

When George was six, the family moved to nearby Ferry Farm and George began to study. He did not like reading and writing, but he loved arithmetic! When he was only 11, his father died. George left school and helped his mother run the farm.

George loved his half-brother Lawrence, who was 13 years older than George. Lawrence taught George how to ride horses, hike in the woods, and work on math and other studies. Lawrence told George many stories of his travels as a soldier.

When George was 16, he got a job **surveying** land. He liked the work, and he liked being in the wild outdoors, riding his horse and sleeping outside.

In 1751, when George was 19, Lawrence got very sick. He went with George to Barbados, a warm tropical island, to try to get well. But Lawrence died there. George decided to be a soldier like his brother.

General George Washington.

Washington the Soldier

When he was only 20, George became a major in the colonial army! This army fought for England, because the colonies were part of England. His first big job was dangerous, but he **volunteered** to do it.

The French built forts in a colony that belonged to England. The army needed a soldier to tell them to go home! George volunteered, and rode to the fort, but the French said they would not leave.

George had an idea. The colonial army could build a fort nearby! This led to a war called the French and Indian War. Many Native Americans, called "Indians" by the colonists, fought on the side of the French because they did not like the colonists moving onto their lands. This is why the war was called the French and Indian War.

English soldiers marched where the enemy could see them. The English thought that to be quiet and to hide was a bad way to fight. But Native Americans were quiet in battle. They slipped behind trees and surprised the English soldiers! In this way, the French and Native Americans won many battles.

As a member of the colonial army, George fought with the English. He lost some battles, but he learned good lessons. The French and Indian War taught him different ways to fight.

Washington praying at Valley Forge during the winter of 1778.

Life at Mt. Vernon

*A*fter the French and Indian War, George went home to Virginia. He had moved to Mt. Vernon in 1748. In 1759, he married Martha Dandridge Custis. Martha's first husband died when she was still young. She had a son, Jack, and a daughter, Patty.

At first, the Washingtons lived in Martha's house. George helped make laws for the new United States. When he wasn't away from home, he and Martha went to parties and dances.

Soon, they moved to George's house, called Mt. Vernon. Mt. Vernon was a **plantation**. At first the plantation grew mostly tobacco. Then George added other crops, like corn and wheat. He knew this was better for the land.

Late in his life, George Washington thought slavery was bad. But most of his life he had slaves. Hundreds of slaves took care of Mt. Vernon. They farmed and gardened. They made tools, shoes, and clothes.

George got up early every morning. He toured the **plantation** on his horse to make sure everything was working. Martha took care of the house. She cooked meals, and she dried fruits from the plantation's many peach, cherry, and apple trees.

Many people came to visit the Washingtons. They had parties and dinners. They listened to music and danced.

George Washington was happy at Mt. Vernon. But in the late 1760s, the United States had more troubles with England. Soon he left Mt. Vernon to work for the new country again.

George Washington and his family.

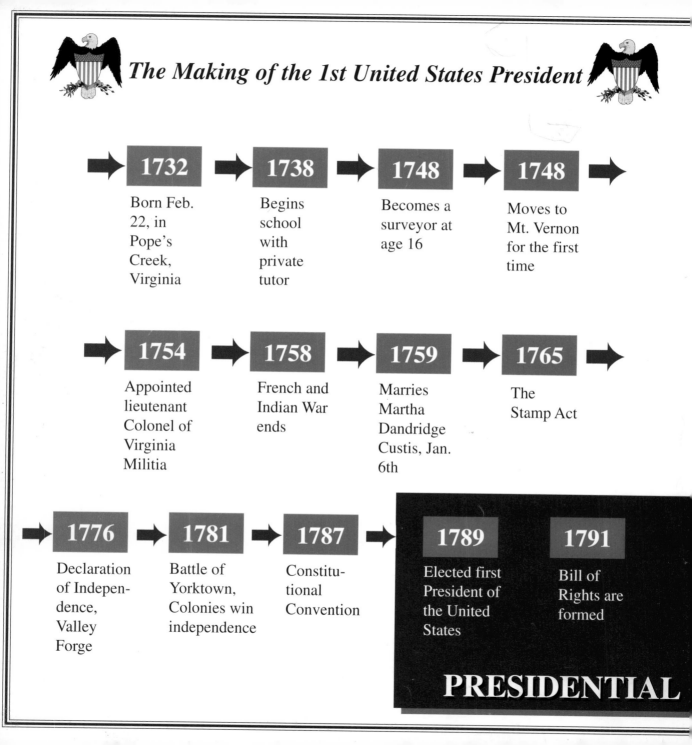

George Washington

"Observe good faith and justice towards all nations, cultivate peace and harmony with all."

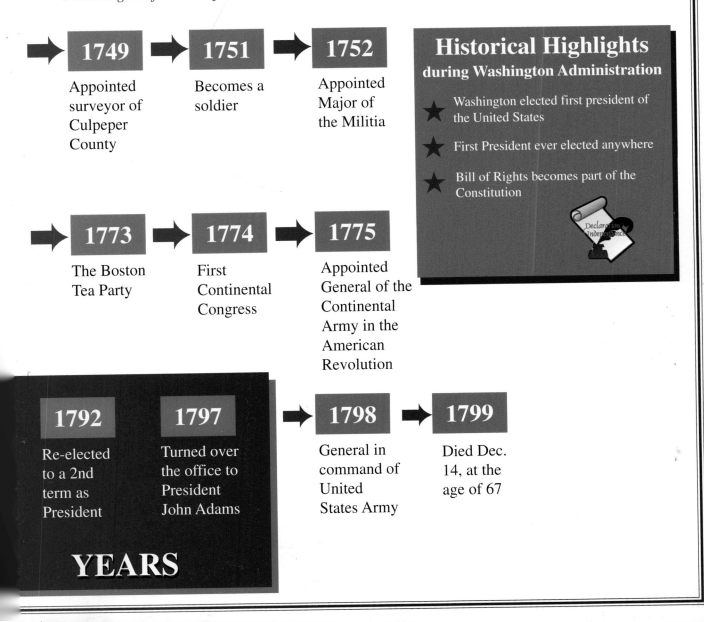

1749
Appointed surveyor of Culpeper County

1751
Becomes a soldier

1752
Appointed Major of the Militia

Historical Highlights
during Washington Administration

★ Washington elected first president of the United States

★ First President ever elected anywhere

★ Bill of Rights becomes part of the Constitution

1773
The Boston Tea Party

1774
First Continental Congress

1775
Appointed General of the Continental Army in the American Revolution

1792
Re-elected to a 2nd term as President

1797
Turned over the office to President John Adams

1798
General in command of United States Army

1799
Died Dec. 14, at the age of 67

YEARS

Leading a Nation to Battle

*I*n the 1760s, the English colonies had to pay many **taxes**. The colonists had to pay high taxes on foods and other goods that they bought from England.

In 1773, colonists climbed onto a ship in Boston Harbor. The ship was full of tea sent from England. The colonists said they would not pay high taxes on the tea anymore. They threw the tea into the ocean! This was called the Boston Tea Party.

In 1774, George Washington and others met to decide what to do. They called themselves the First Continental **Congress**. The men picked George Washington to lead the Congress.

The English knew the colonists were not happy. They had soldiers in the colonies called **redcoats**, because their uniforms were long, red coats. The colonists had soldiers, too. They were called **minutemen** because they traveled quickly from place to place. They did this to warn colonists when the **redcoats** were coming.

In April 1775, English soldiers shot and killed 18 colonists. **Minutemen** fought back. This began the American **Revolution**.

Soon the **Congress** met again. They needed a General to lead the army. They all chose George Washington. He and his men began the fight for freedom from England.

General George Washington leads the siege of Yorktown.

A General and a President

*A*bout one year later, on July 4, 1776, **Congress** signed a paper called the **Declaration of Independence**. The paper said the colonies wanted to be free.

That fall, the **redcoats** killed many American soldiers in a big battle. George Washington and his men had to **retreat** across the Delaware River.

But he had a plan. On December 25, 1776, Christmas Day, the redcoats rested and celebrated the holiday. That night, George Washington and his men crossed the Delaware again. They traveled through cold and snow to the redcoats' camp and surrounded them. The redcoats were so surprised that they lost the battle! A few days later, they lost another battle, too.

The winter of 1777 was very cold. The soldiers sometimes were hungry, and many died. Martha Washington stayed with them at Valley Forge and cooked hot food.

The war dragged on for many years. Summers were hot and winters were cold. Soldiers sometimes lost hope. George Washington talked to them to try to keep their hopes up.

Other countries watched to see who would win. In 1781, French soldiers came to help the Americans win a big battle at Yorktown. With this battle, in the fall of 1781, the colonists won the American **Revolution**!

But there was still much work to do. Many soldiers had no money. Now with the end of the war, they had no jobs, either.

The soldiers wanted George Washington to take over and be king! He told them he would not. He reminded them that this was what the fighting was all about!

In 1783, George Washington went home to Mt. Vernon. He and Martha spent many years at home. He was 51 years old. By this time, he wore glasses and false teeth.

He traveled and tried new ways of farming his land. He liked being home again. But the United States of America had new problems. The laws were not strong enough.

In 1787, there was another meeting, called a **convention**, to make up a new, stronger law for the United States. Each state sent a person, called a delegate. Virginia sent George Washington.

When the convention started, the other delegates picked George Washington to be its president! They wrote a paper called the **Constitution**. It described what the United States stood for and listed new laws.

Next, the new United States voted for its first president! George Washington got the most votes. He was the first president of the new United States. He had to decide for himself what a president should do.

Washington at his inauguration on April 30, 1789.

The President's Work

*G*eorge Washington served two terms as president. Each term lasted four years. This is the same with presidents today.

In his first term, George Washington helped pass an important paper called the **Bill of Rights**. This added ten rights to the **Constitution**. One of these is freedom of speech, the right to say what you believe in. Another is freedom of religion, the right to worship however you want.

Every American votes for, or elects, the people in the government. This form of government is called a democracy. George Washington worked to build this government.

The **Congress** formed new groups in the government, called departments. George Washington then picked people to head these departments. They were called the **cabinet**. These departments and the cabinet are still part of our government today.

George Washington also helped to plan a new capital city for the United States. At that time, the United States capital moved around the country. It was in New York City, Philadelphia, and other places.

George Washington picked a spot near the Potomac River. Many new buildings were planned for this new capital. When it was finished the capital was named after him. It is Washington, D.C.

In 1792, George Washington was elected to a second term. France was in a war in Europe. Because France helped America in its American **Revolution**, it now wanted the United States to help it in return.

But George Washington would not help. He believed the new country was still too weak, and had too many problems to fix at home. Many people did not agree with his decision.

He also had more troubles with England. England stopped America's ships and broke rules about how to buy and sell things between countries. George Washington took a long time to think about how to deal with these problems. Once again, many people did not agree with his decisions.

Many people still liked George Washington. They wanted him to run for a third term. But he had enough! He retired in 1796 and went home to Mt. Vernon.

Washington presiding in the Constitutional Convention in 1787.

No Place Like Home

While he was President, George Washington had many parties. Many people came to his home to visit, listen to music, and share meals. He had really big parties for his birthdays!

The visits continued when he went home to Mt. Vernon. So many people came that George and Martha did not have dinner alone for many weeks after they returned!

While he was president, George adopted two of Martha's grandchildren, Eleanor and George. Now they were part of home life, too. George rode his horse through the big **plantation**, wrote letters, and rested. He was older and got tired sooner.

There were still many troubles between the United States and France. In 1798, President John Adams decided the United States needed a bigger army to protect it. He asked George to help build that army.

George Washington worked for a short time to help plan the army. He visited friends. Then he returned to Mt. Vernon.

One winter day he rode his horse in heavy snow. He got cold and wet, and became very sick. On December 14, 1799, he died. People from all over the world were sad at his death. Many U.S. citizens wore black clothing for many months.

Today, many towns, parks, schools, and streets are named after George Washington. He is still honored as the father of our country.

George Washington with his horse.

A Man Named George Washington

•In his studies, George Washington hated spelling! Sometimes a word that sounds one way is spelled another. George did not like that. He told his teacher that words should look the way they sound. In one lesson, George spelled 14 out of 20 words wrong!

•George Washington had many sets of false teeth. One of them was made of wood! He was shy about his false teeth. For this reason, he closed his mouth tightly when his pictures were painted. This is why he sometimes looks stern in his pictures.

•George Washington was born on February 11, 1732. But in 1753, a new calendar was used. This changed the dates, and his birthday became February 22.

•George Washington was shy in front of groups. When he tried to give his first big speech, his face turned red, he spoke so softly nobody could hear him, and he stammered. Later he got better at giving speeches. But he never liked it.

•George and Martha Washington had early bed-times for grown-ups. They went to bed at about nine p.m.

•George Washington was the best wrestler in his class. He also was good at pole vaulting, horse riding, and shooting.

•When George Washington was a little boy, he had no one to play with except his sister and brother. They lived where there were no other people for miles and miles! He rode his pony and explored the woods near his house. Later, the family moved to another place so George and his brothers and sisters could go to school.

Washington kept his mouth closed so his false teeth wouldn't show.

Glossary

Bill of Rights—an important paper that lists ten rights that belong to all Americans; it is part of the Constitution.

Cabinet—one group of people in the United States government; the Cabinet is picked by the President.

Congress—one group of people in the United States government; the Congress helps decide laws, and members of Congress are elected by U.S. citizens.

Constitution—an important piece of paper that describes freedom and rights for Americans.

Convention—a big meeting.

Declaration of Independence—an important paper that said the English colonies wanted to be free and start their own government.

Minutemen—colonists who helped fight the English in the American Revolution; they traveled quickly from place to place to warn colonists that English soldiers were coming.

Plantation—a big farm.

Redcoats—nickname for English soldiers, who wore long, red uniforms.

Retreat—to go back.

Revolution—the American Revolution was a war that happened because Americans wanted their own country, free from England.

Surveyor—a person who surveys, or measures, land and points out where the borders are.

Taxes—extra fees paid to the government.

Volunteer—to do something without being asked or told.

Internet Sites

The Presidents of the United States of America
http://www.whitehouse.gov/WH/glimpse/presidents/html/presidents.html
This site is from the White House. With an introduction from President Bill Clinton and biographies that include each president's inaugural address, this site is excellent. Get White House History information, Art in the White House, First Ladies, First Families, and much more.

POTUS—Presidents of the United States
http://www.ipl.org/ref/POTUS/
In this resource you will find background information, election results, cabinet members, presidency highlights, and some odd facts on each of the presidents. Links to biographies, historical documents, audio and video files, and other presidential sites are also included to enrich this site.

These sites are subject to change. Go to your favorite search engine and type in United States Presidents for more sites.

Pass It On

History Enthusiasts: educate readers around the country by passing on information you've learned about Presidents or other important people who've changed history. Share your little-known facts and interesting stories. We want to hear from you!

To get posted on the ABDO Publishing Company website E-mail us at "History@abdopub.com"
Visit the ABDO Publishing Company website at www.abdopub.com

Index